CALM

Cynthia Morel-Pence

Calm
Copyright © 2023 by Cynthia Morel-Pence

All rights reserved. No part of this publication may be reproduced, distributed, or transmitted in any form or by any means, including photocopying, recording, or other electronic or mechanical methods, without the prior written permission of the author, except in the case of brief quotations embodied in critical reviews and certain other non-commercial uses permitted by copyright law.

Tellwell Talent
www.tellwell.ca

ISBN
978-0-2288-8060-8 (Hardcover)
978-0-2288-8059-2 (Paperback)

Sometimes when I get in trouble I feel sad.

Other times, things sometimes happen and it makes me feel really mad.

One day a nice yoga teacher came to our school. She taught us all how to breathe and calm ourselves when we are feeling sad or mad, and it was really easy and very cool.

My teacher said you pretend to breathe IN pretty flowers, that smell so nice to your nose. Then all you have to do is breathe OUT your mouth and really let it blow!!

Whenever I feel sad or mad or someone isn't nice to me, or says something mean. I can do this deep breathing and calm myself and soon I feel relaxed and serene.

This breathing calms me right away. I've also learned how to take a break from playing and talking with my friends any time of day.

My yoga teacher taught me that mindful breathing calms the body and positive thoughts calm the mind. I just think happy thoughts and take deep breaths and then my heart starts to feel relaxed and kind. These are such easy things to do. I hope that you will join me and feel wonderful and calm too!

THE END

Printed in the USA
CPSIA information can be obtained
at www.ICGtesting.com
LVHW070802030923
757071LV00015B/150